I0472090

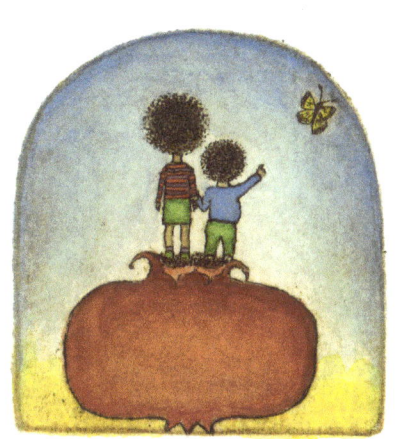

*Dedicated to the honor*
*that it is in raising*
*my two beautifuls...*
*big sister*
*and*
*baby brother*

One day,
my princess,
you will stand
on a great big
pomegranate
and will look
right at the
castle
that will someday
be your home.

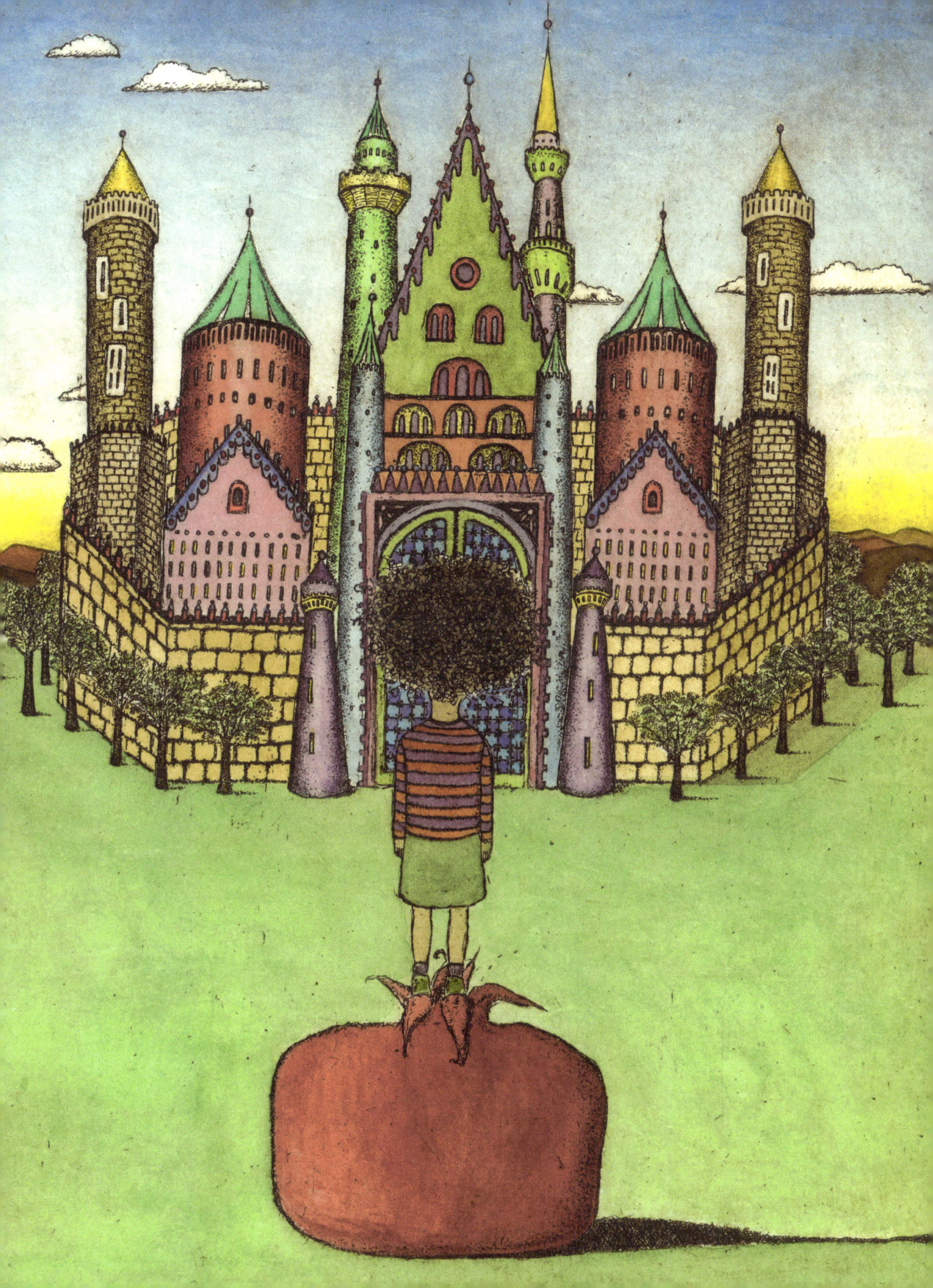

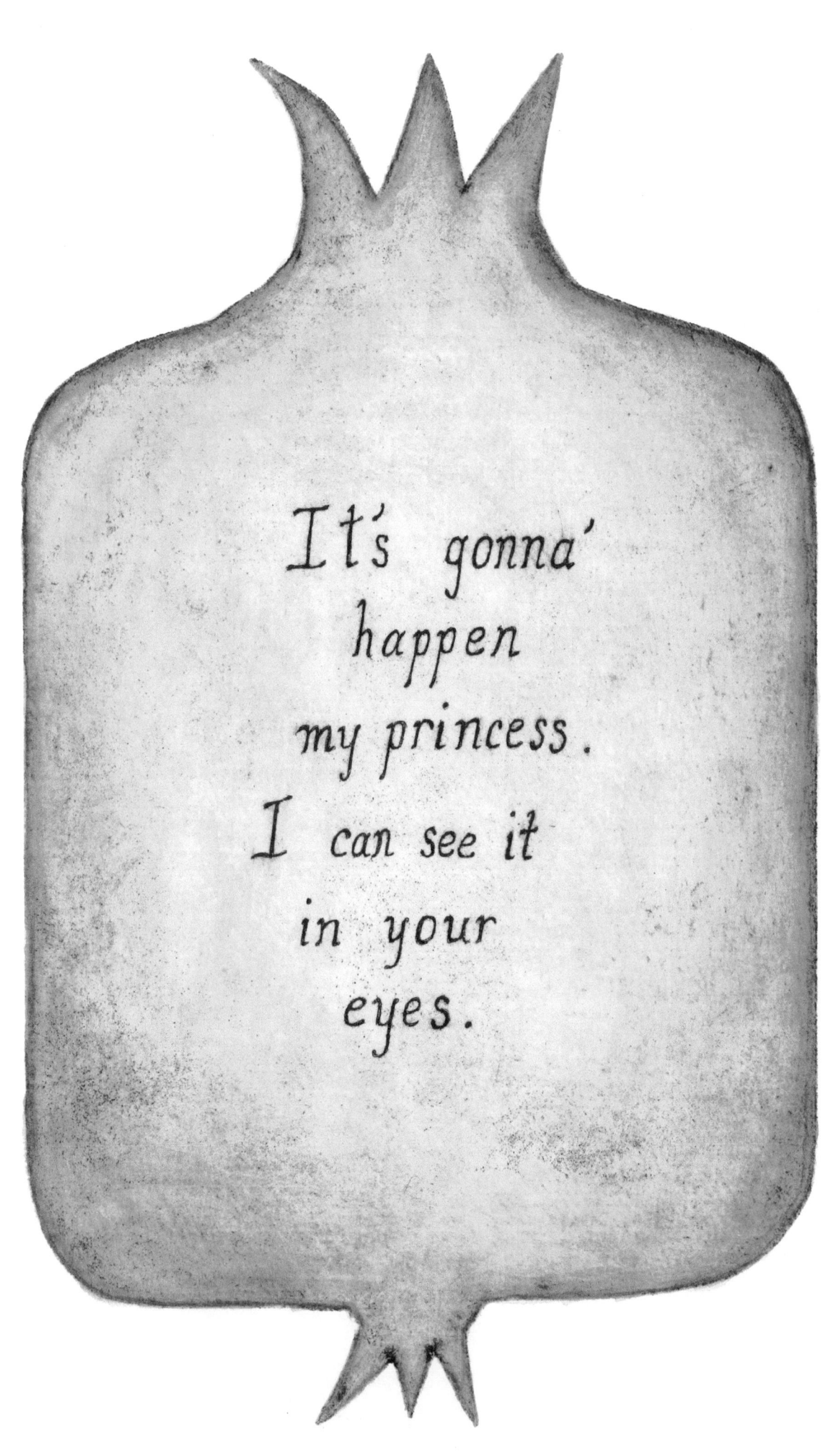

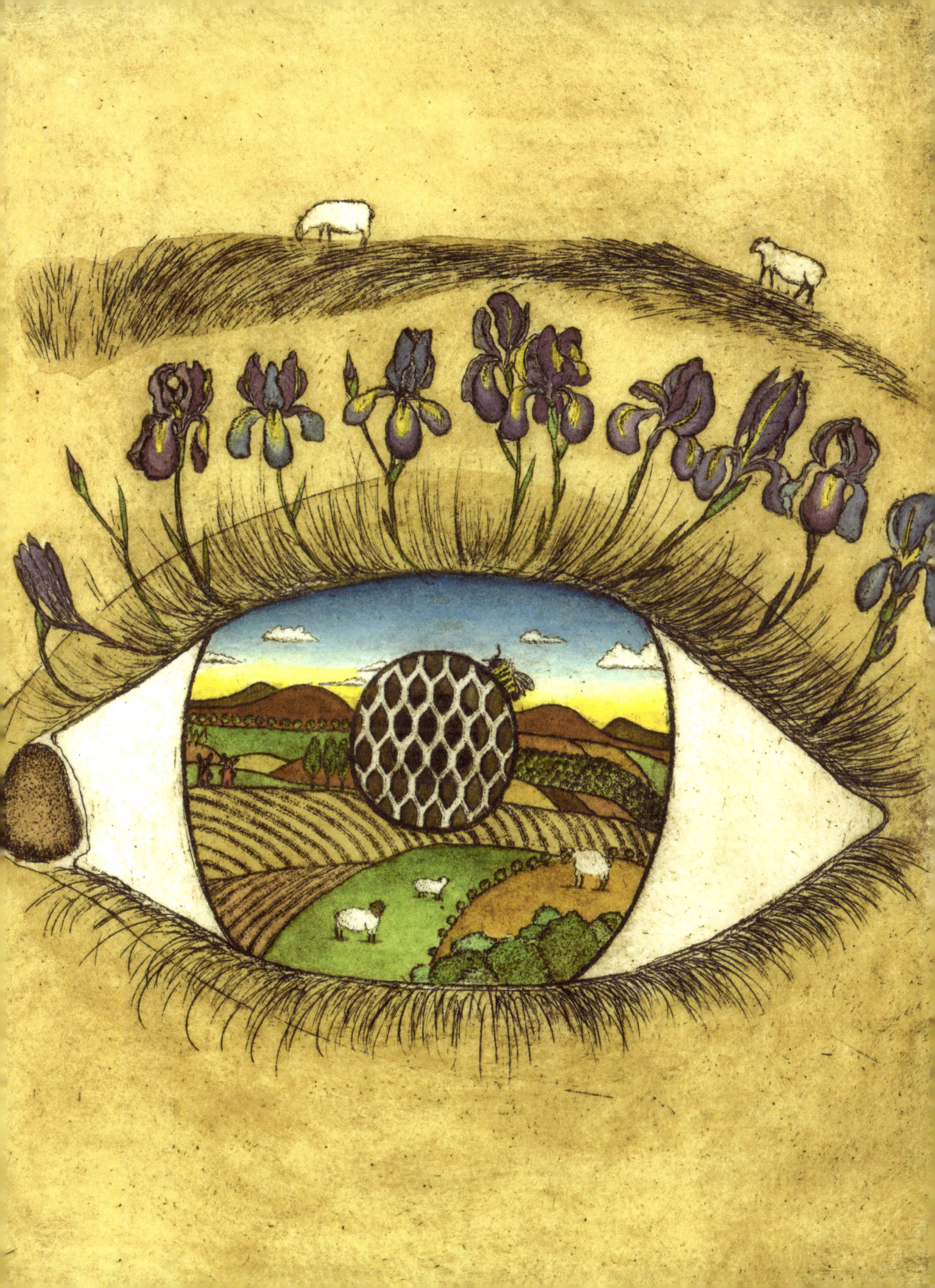

As the
clear
blue  sky opens up
and
from inside of it
fly out
all
the singing birds
and
dancing butterflies,

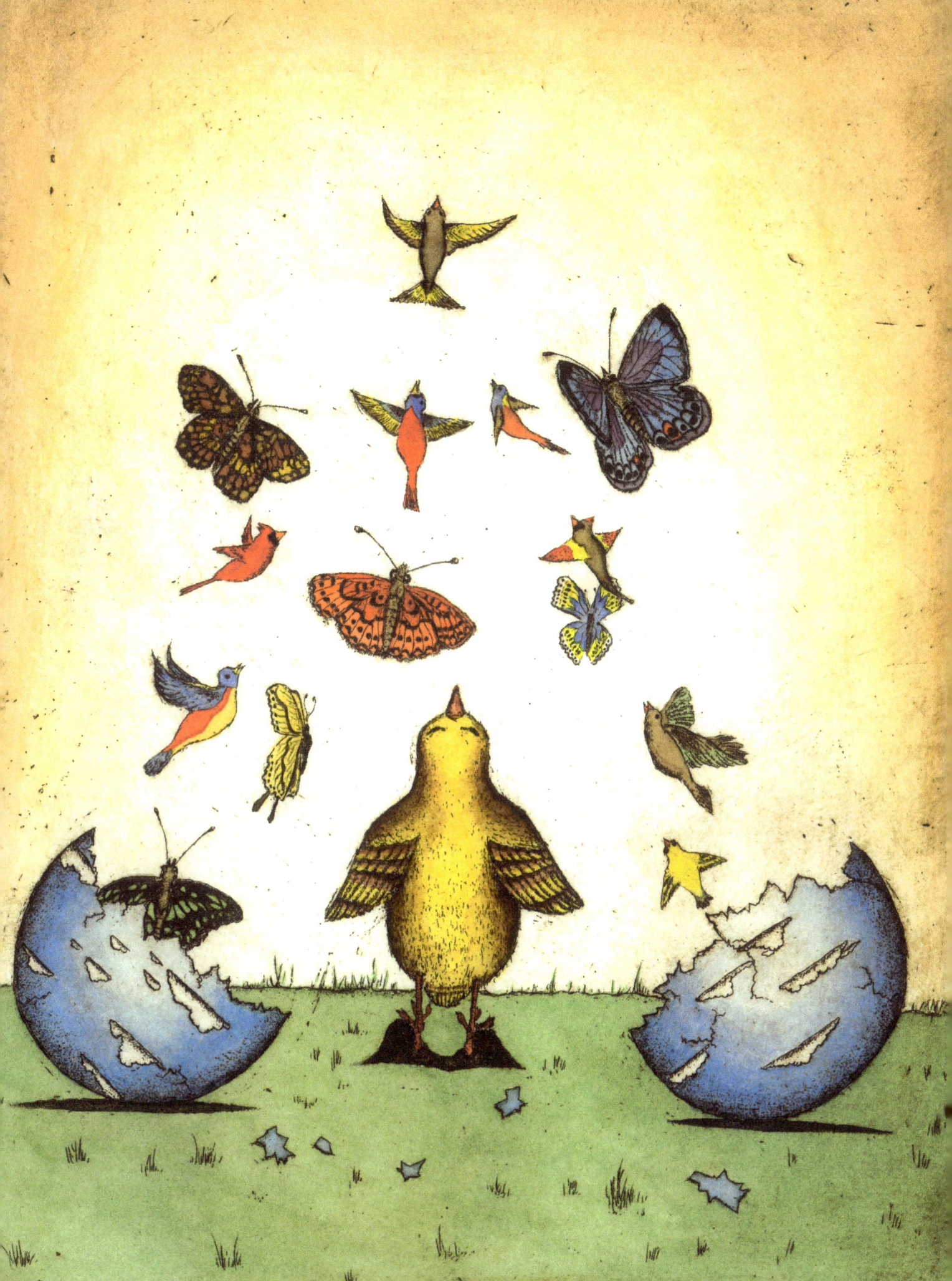

and as the
bees buzz
all around
showering the earth
with
lots and lots
of
golden honey,

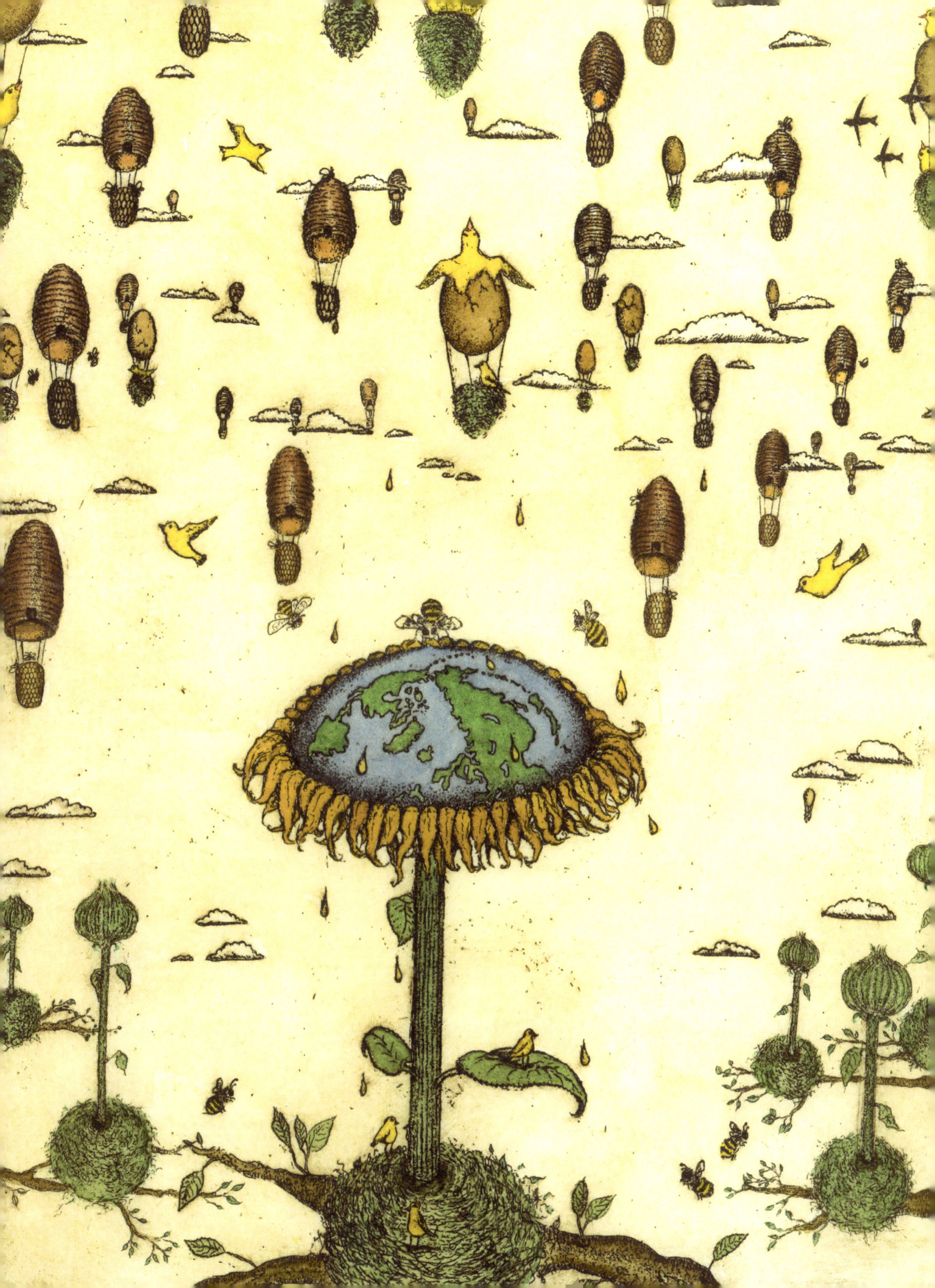

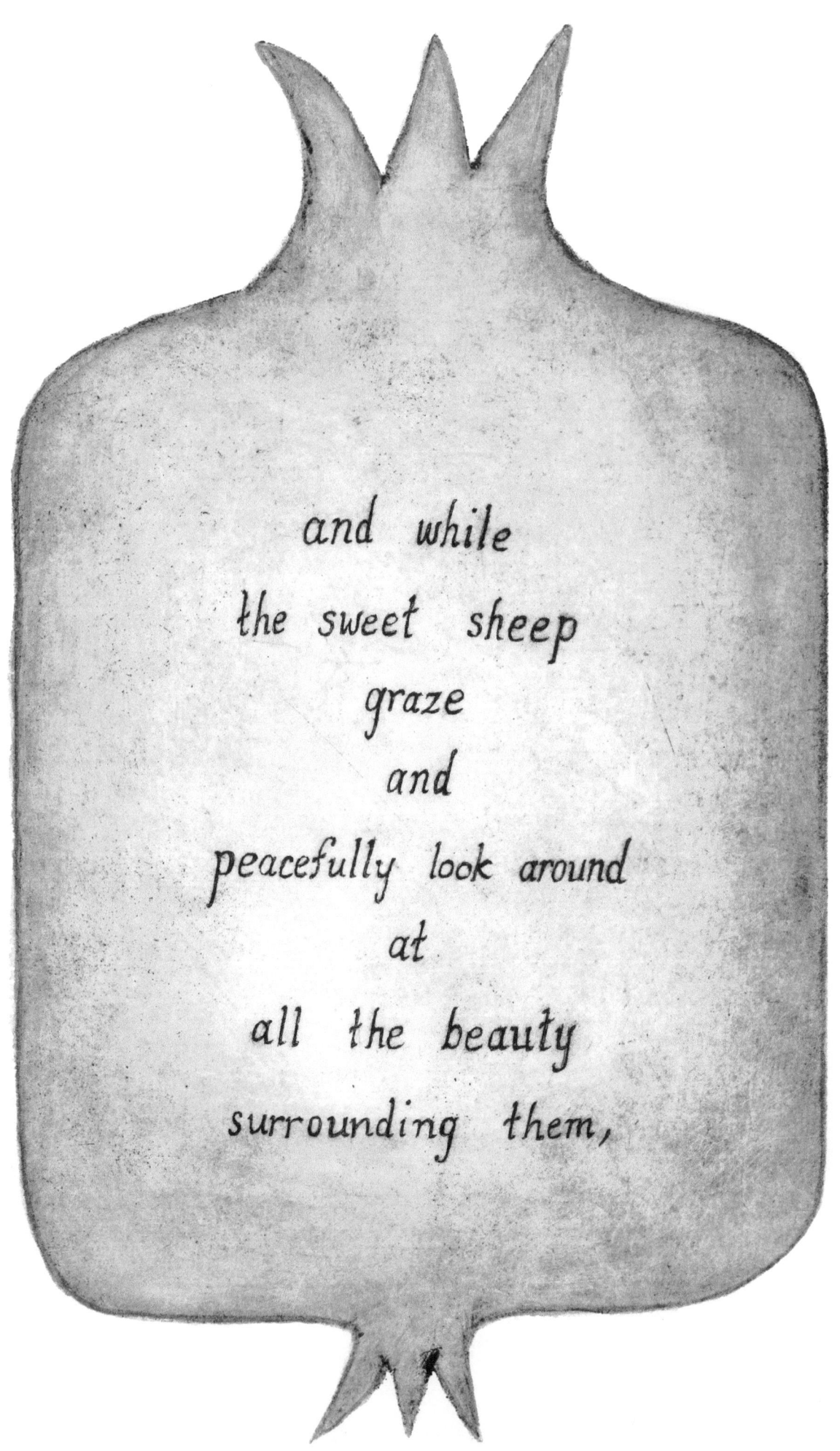

and while

the sweet sheep

graze

and

peacefully look around

at

all the beauty

surrounding them,

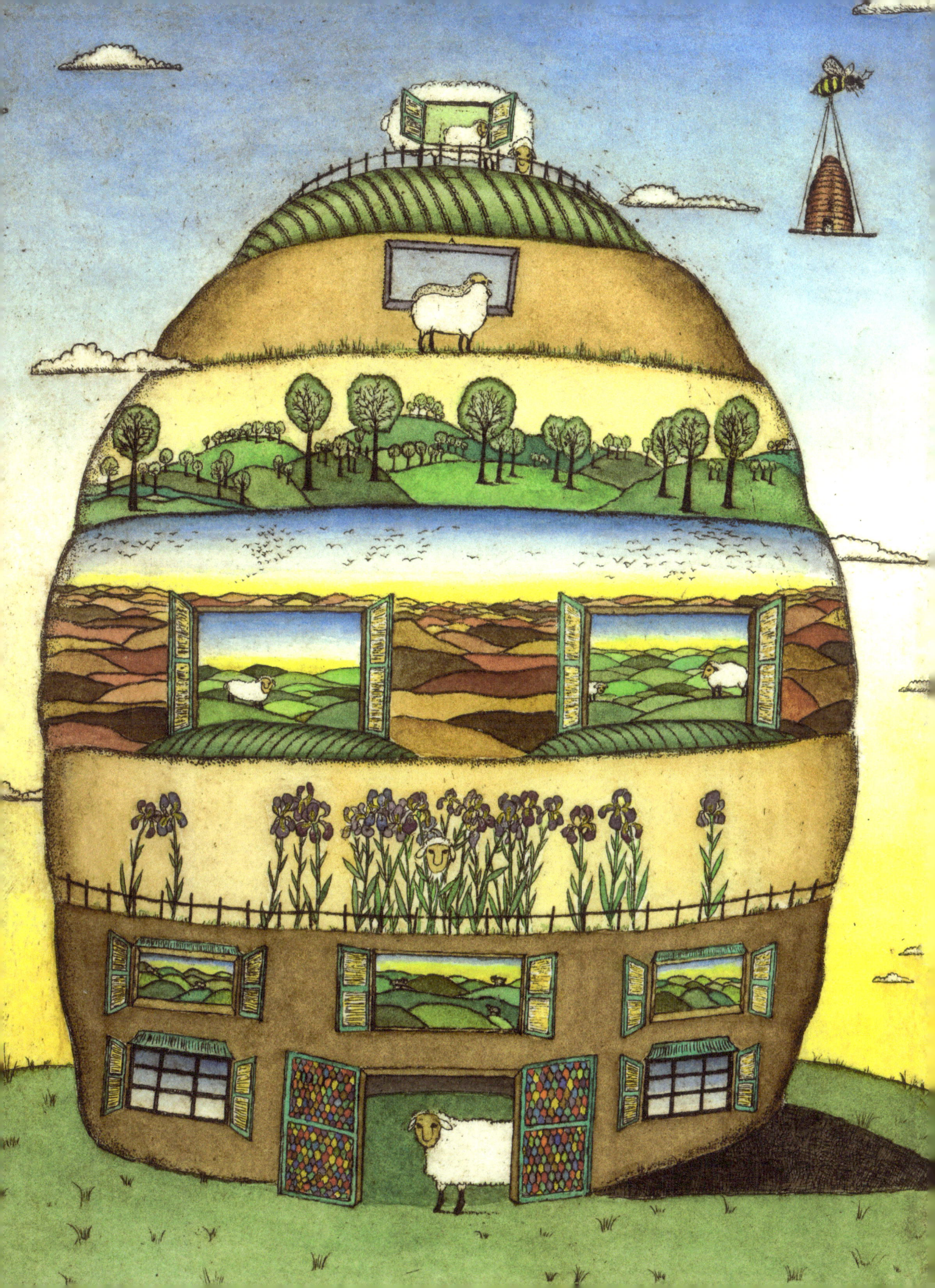

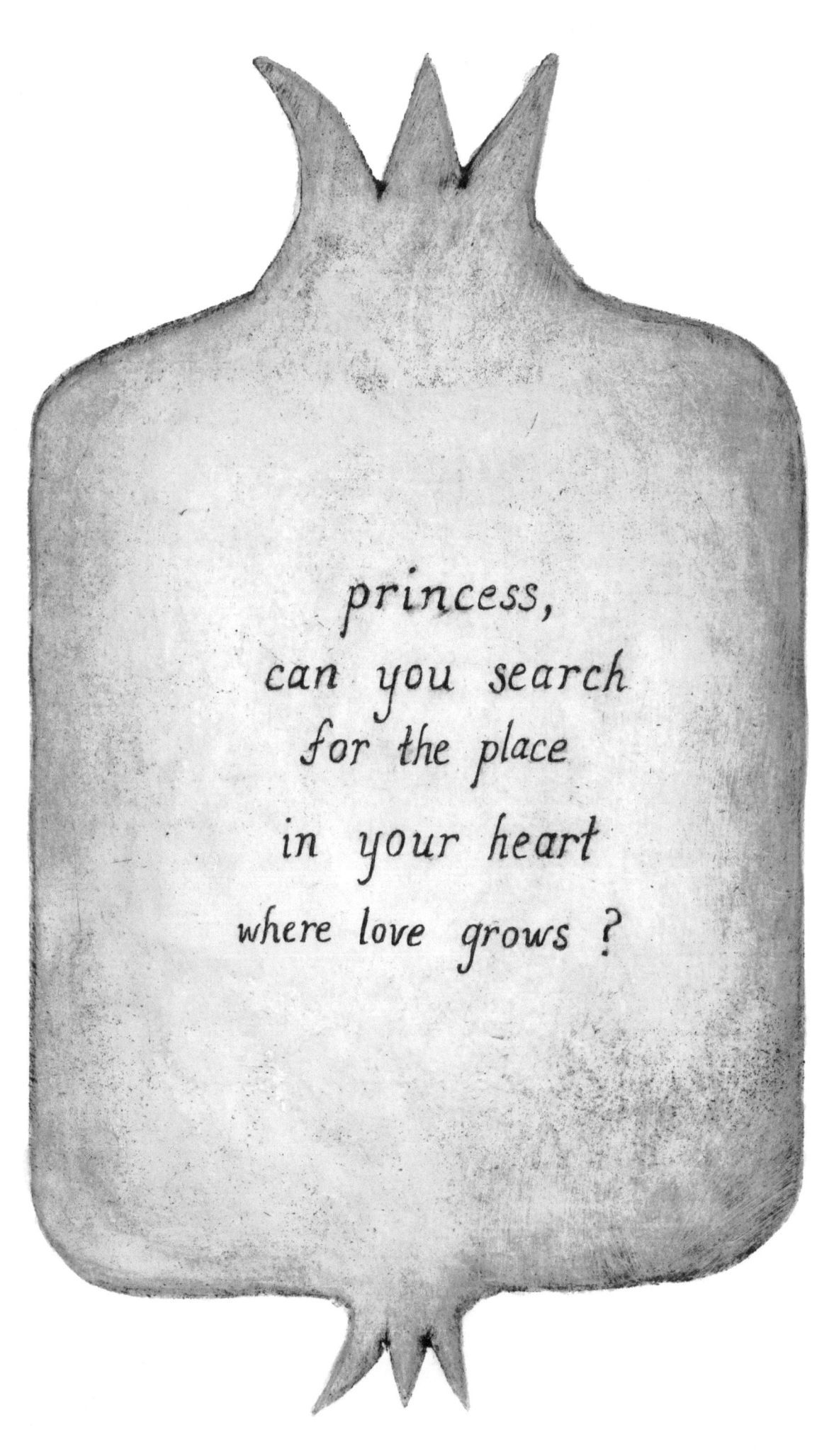

princess,
can you search
for the place

in your heart

where love grows?

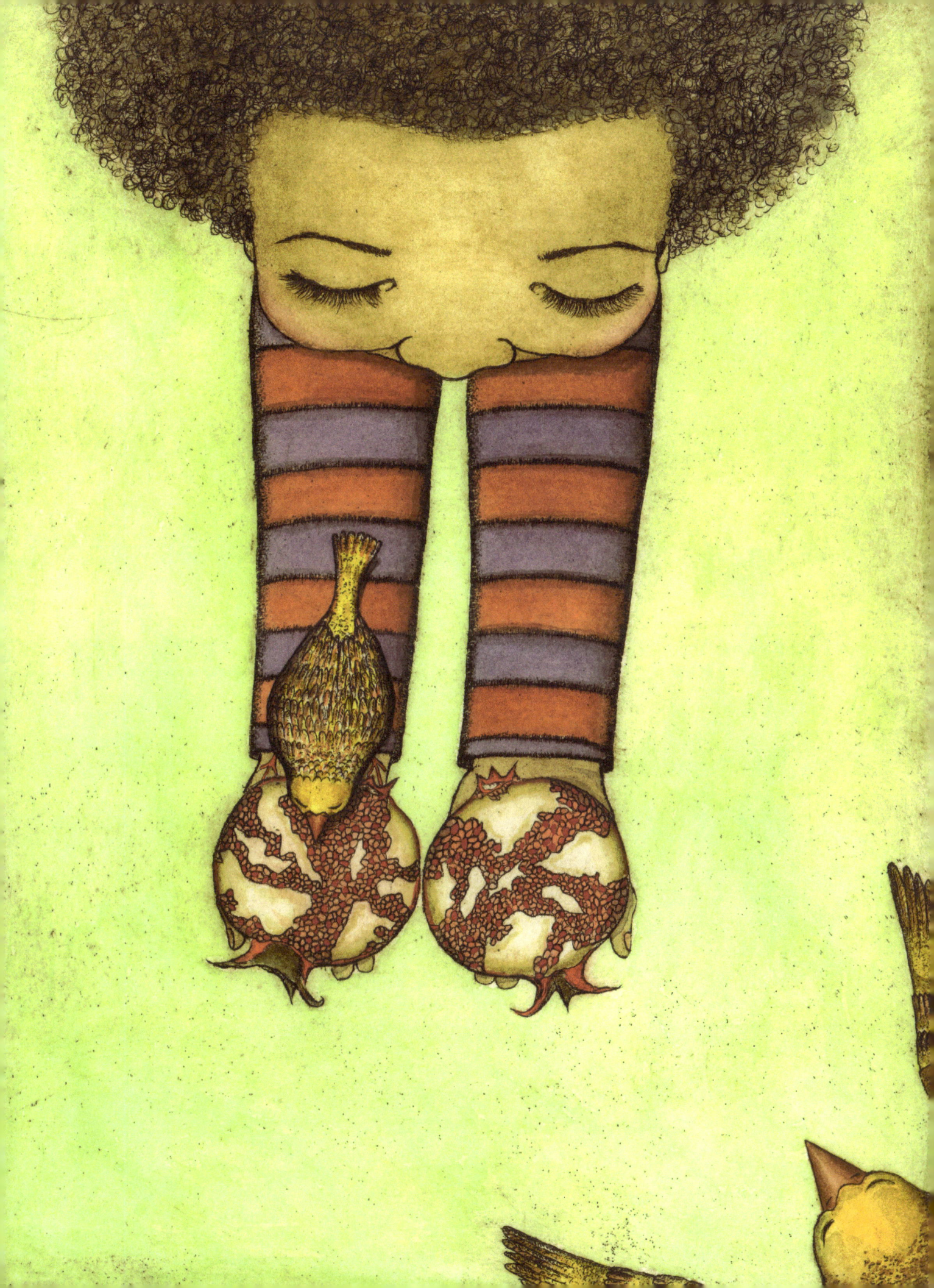

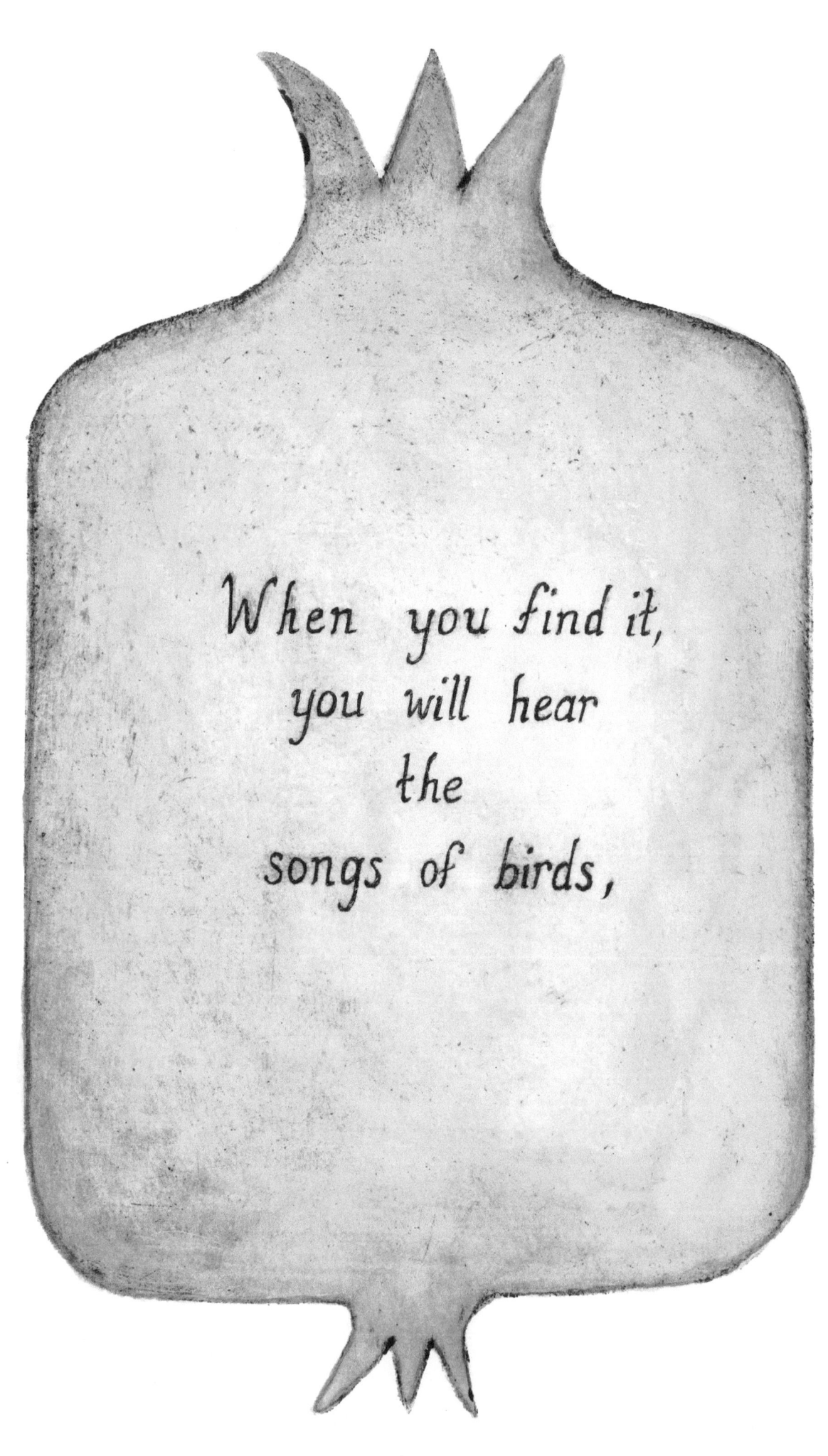

When you find it,
you will hear
the
songs of birds,

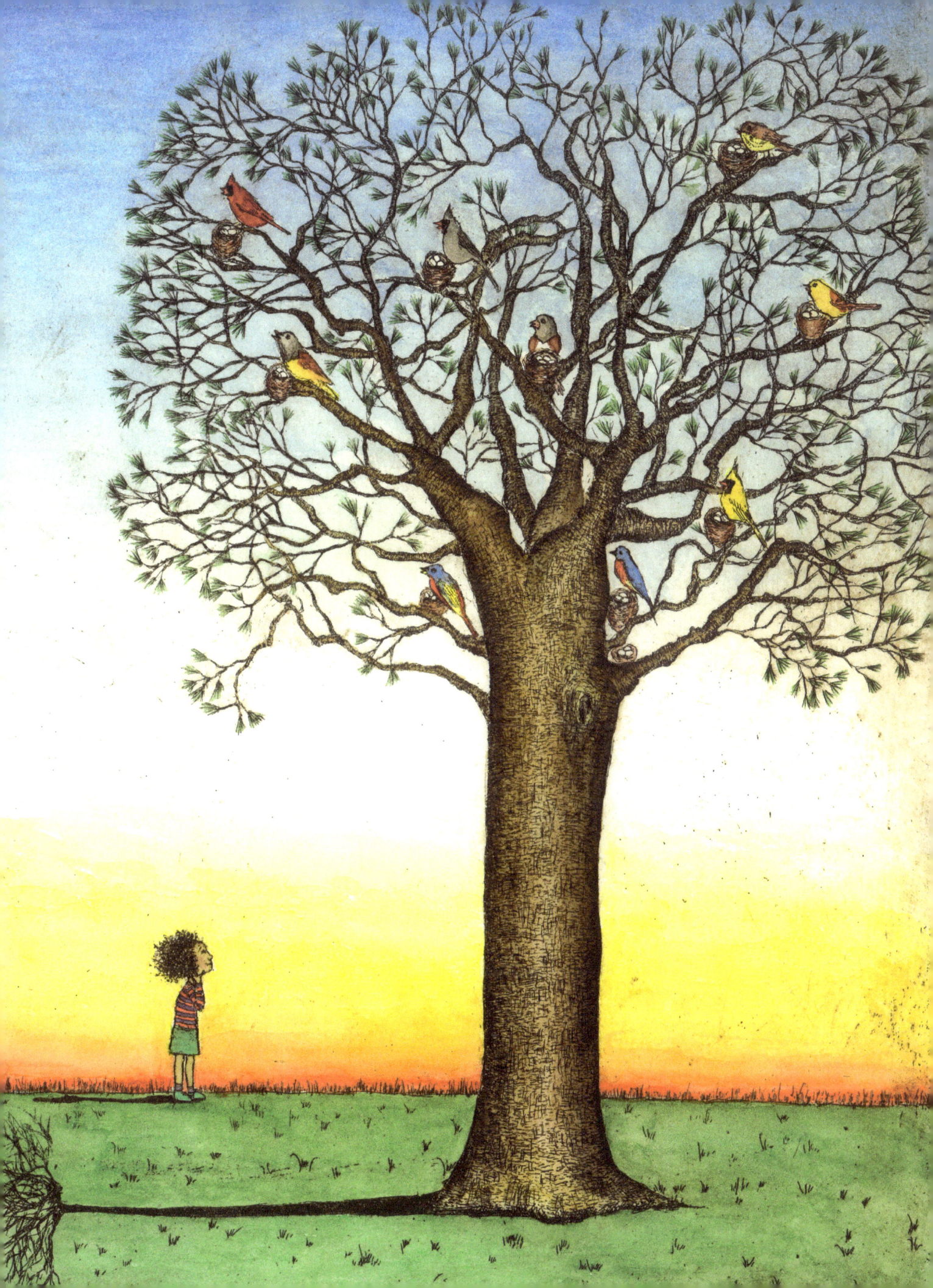

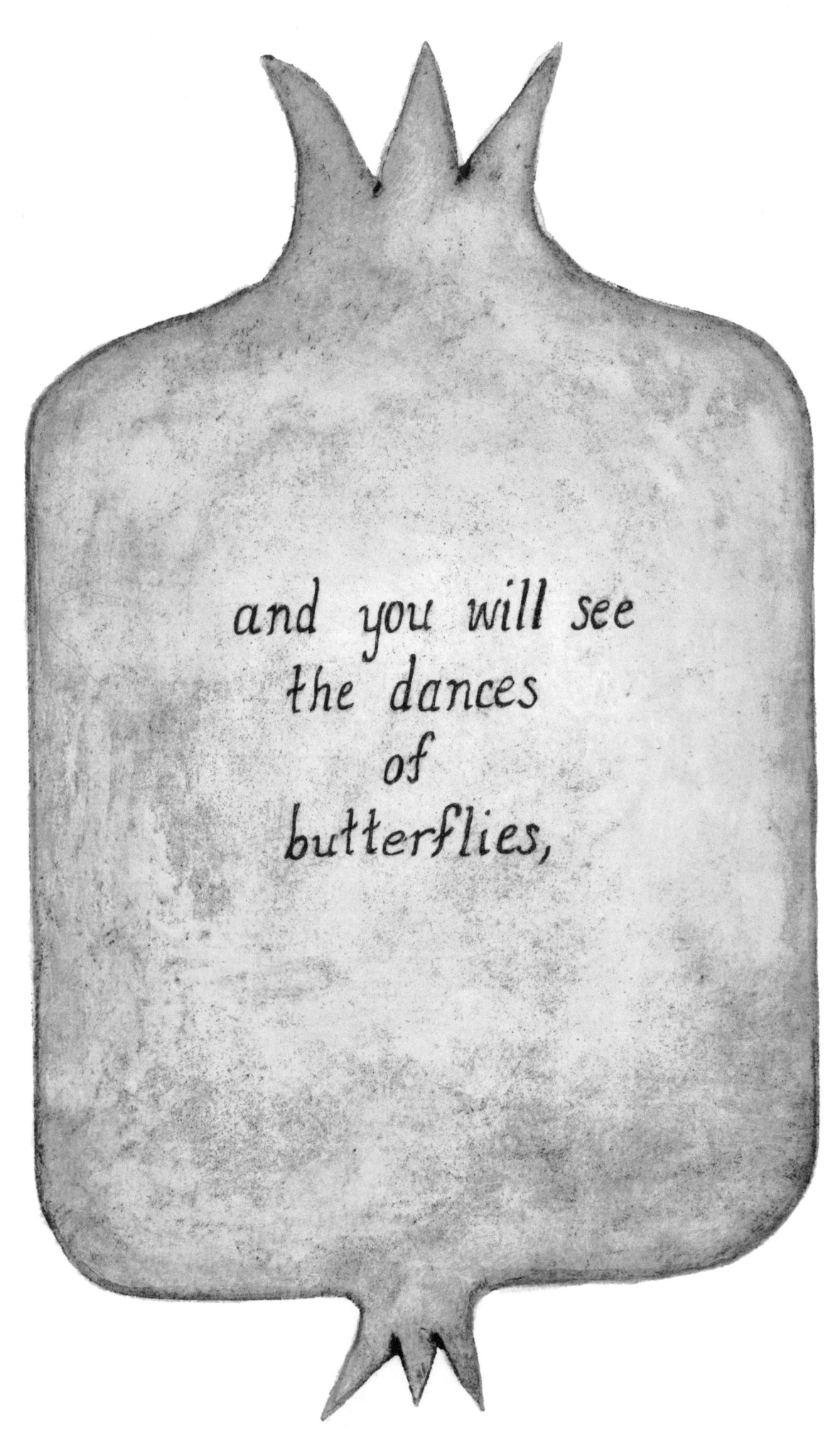

and you will see
the dances
of
butterflies,

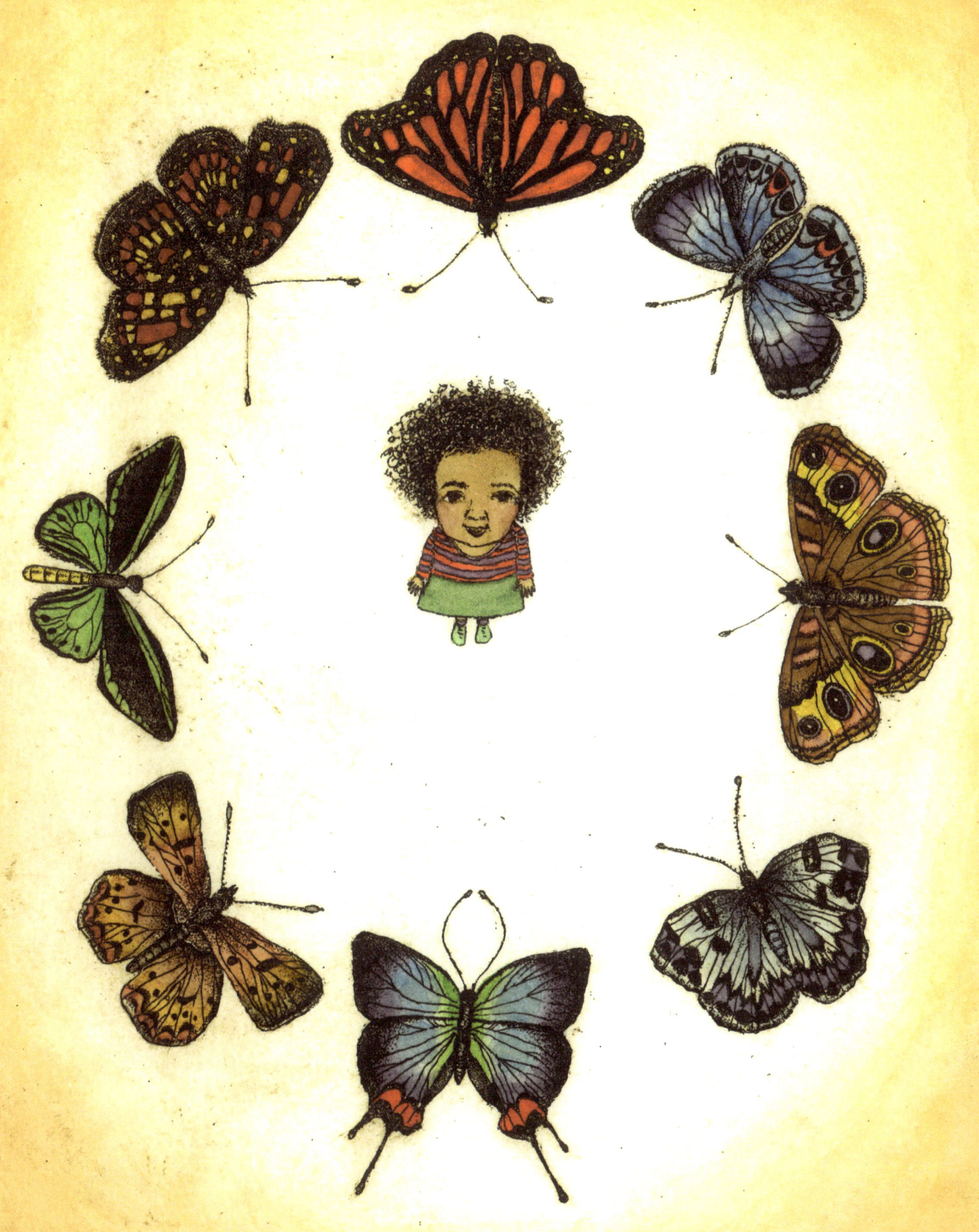

and you will taste
the honey
from
bee hives,

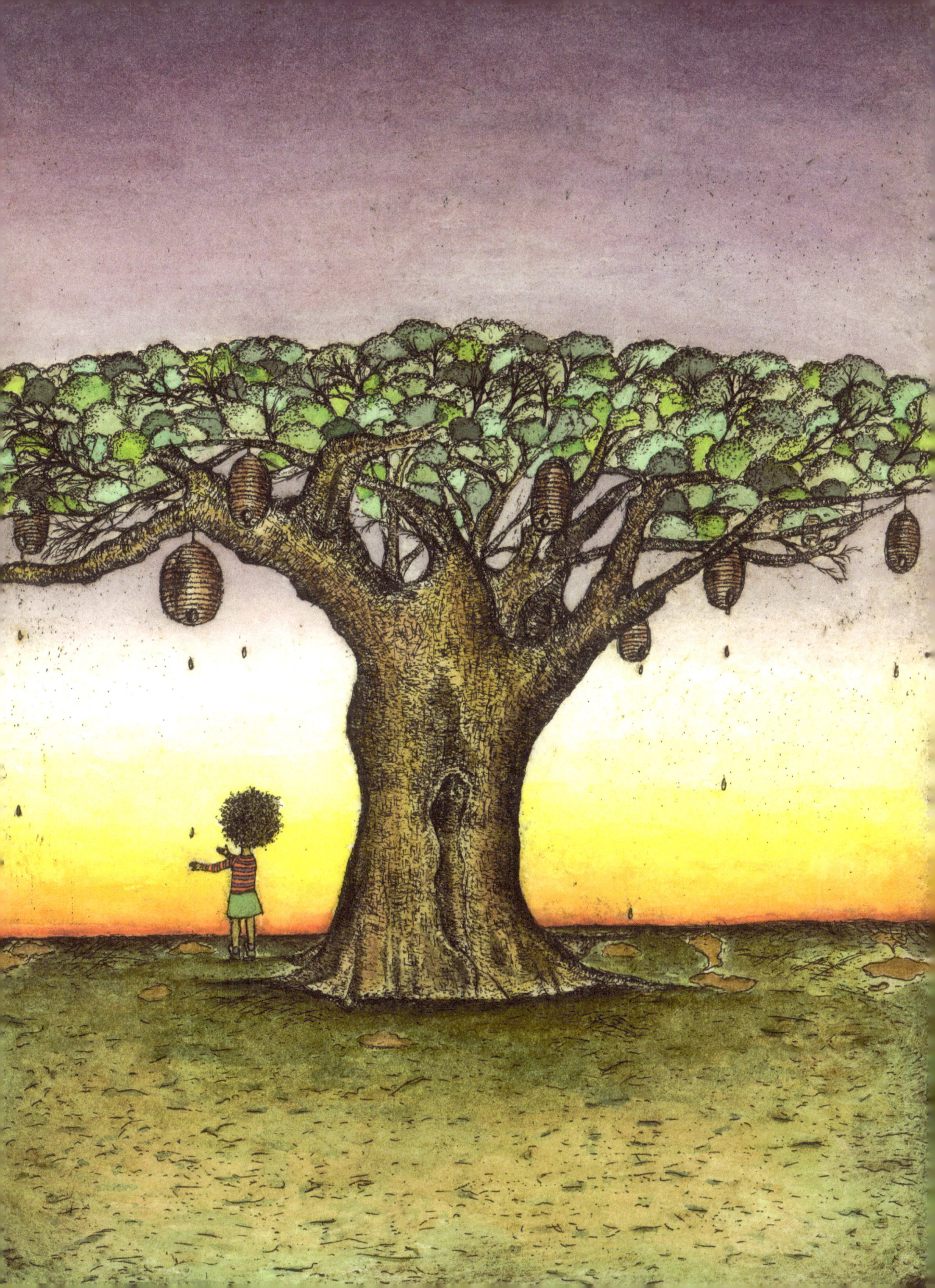

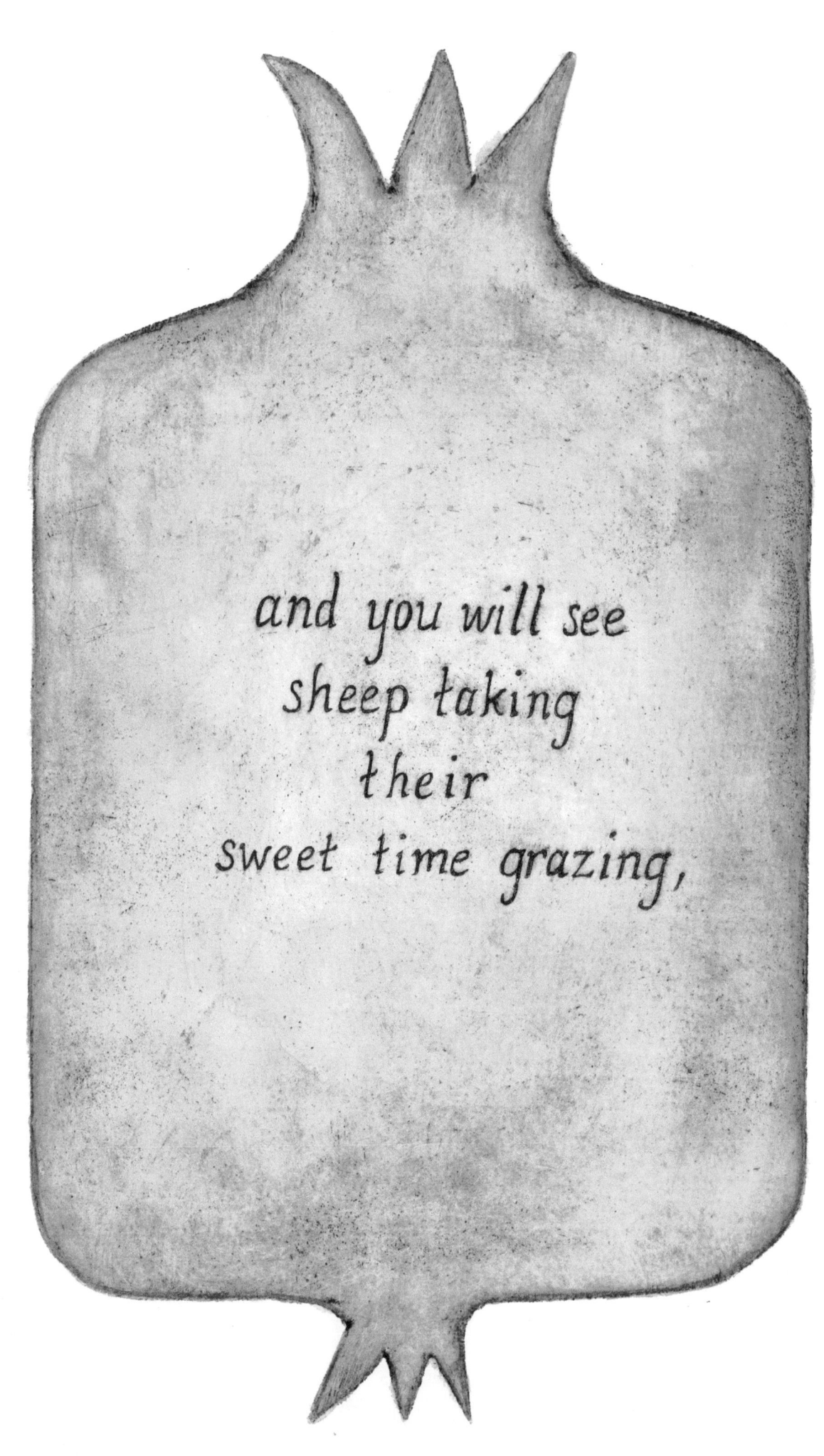

and you will see
sheep taking
their
sweet time grazing,

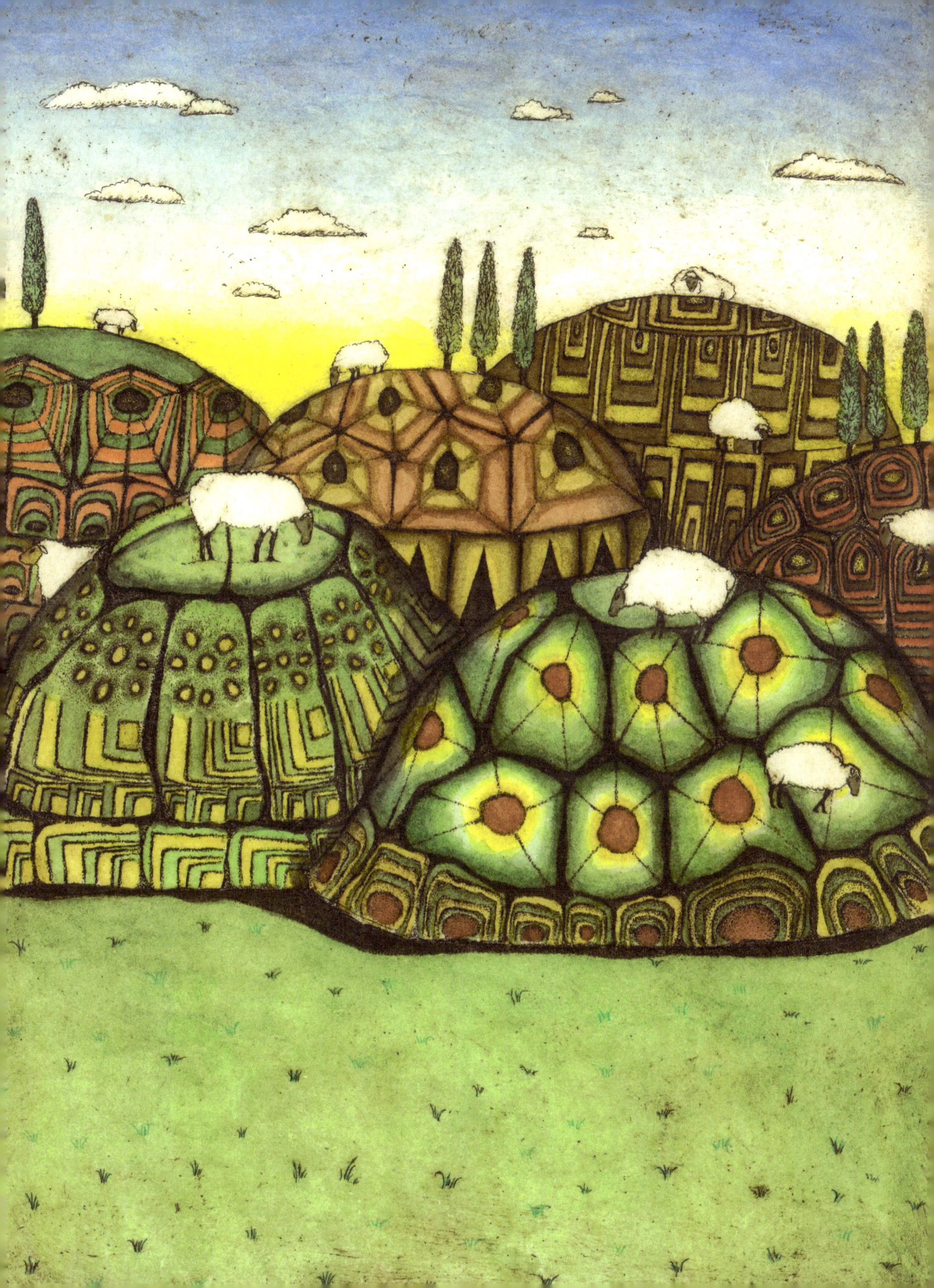

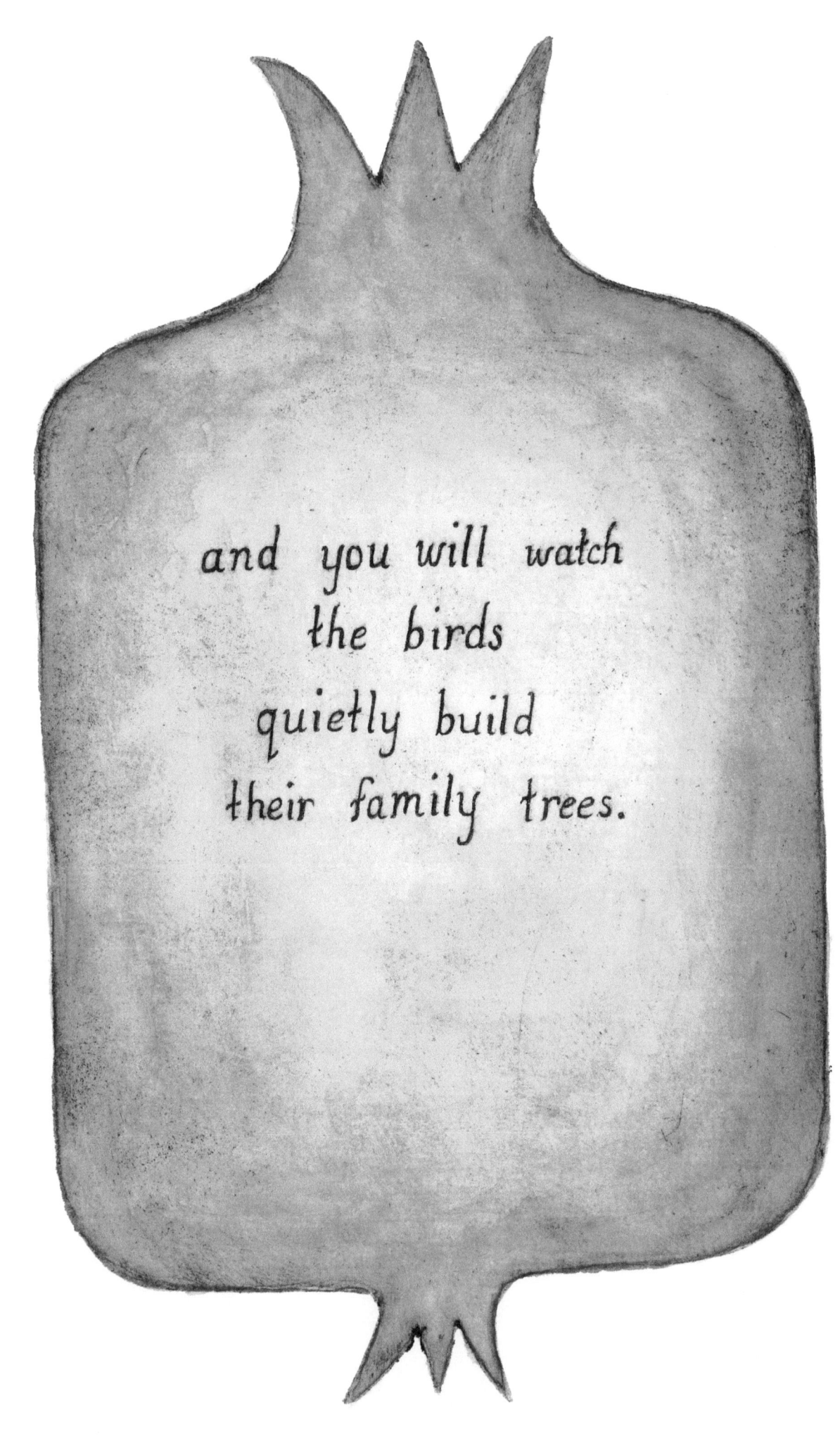

and you will watch
the birds
quietly build
their family trees.

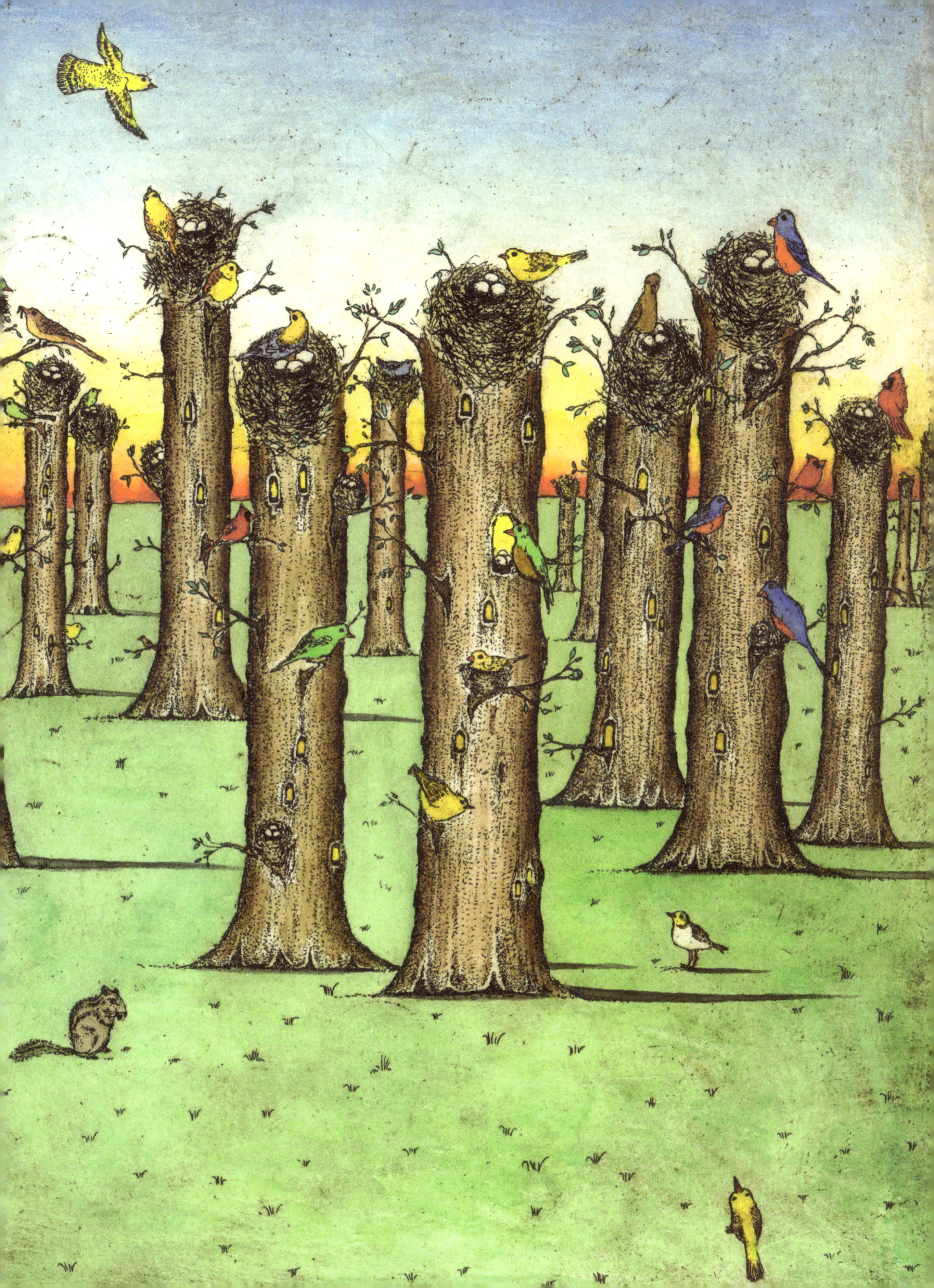

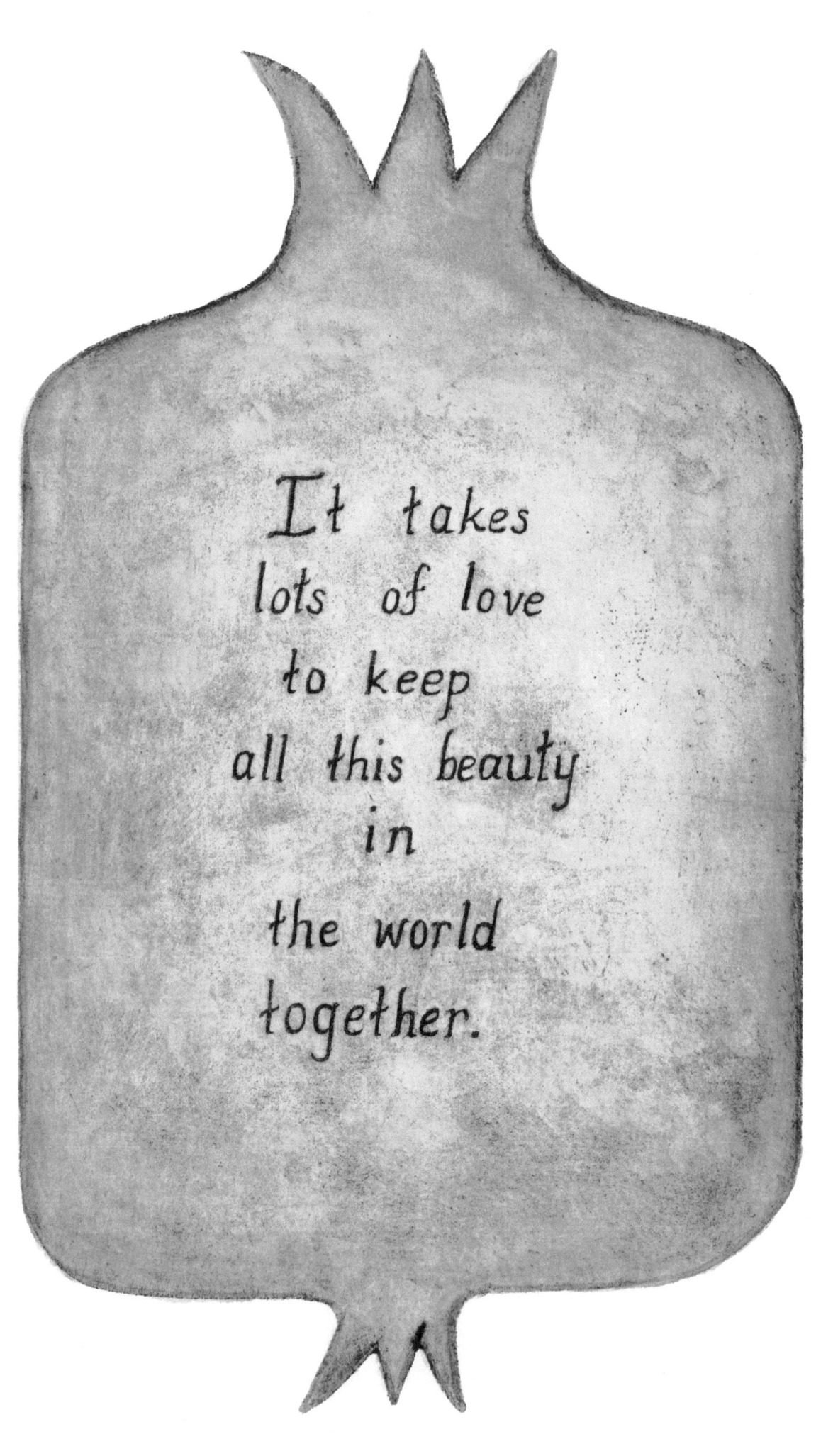

It takes
lots of love
to keep
all this beauty
in
the world
together.

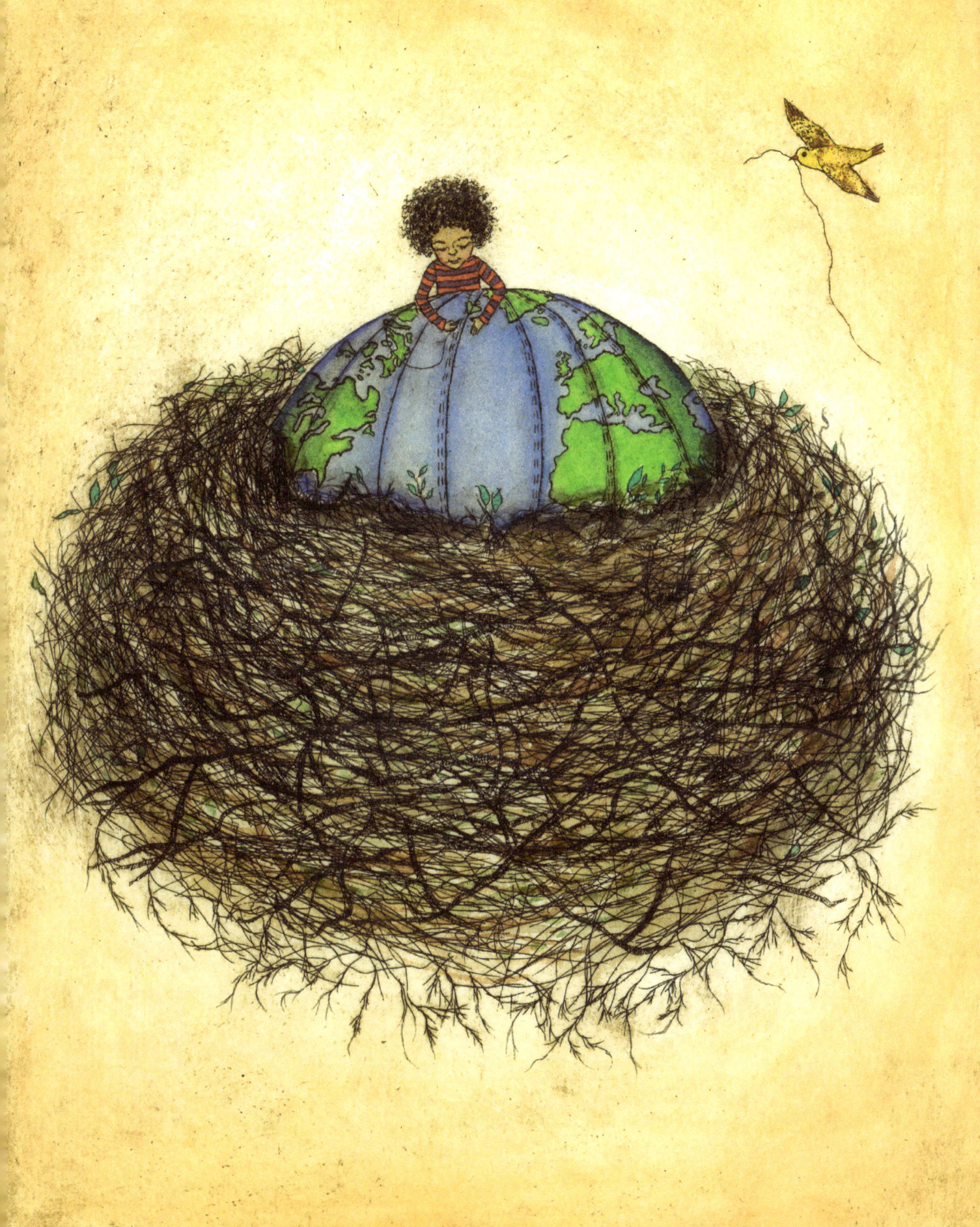

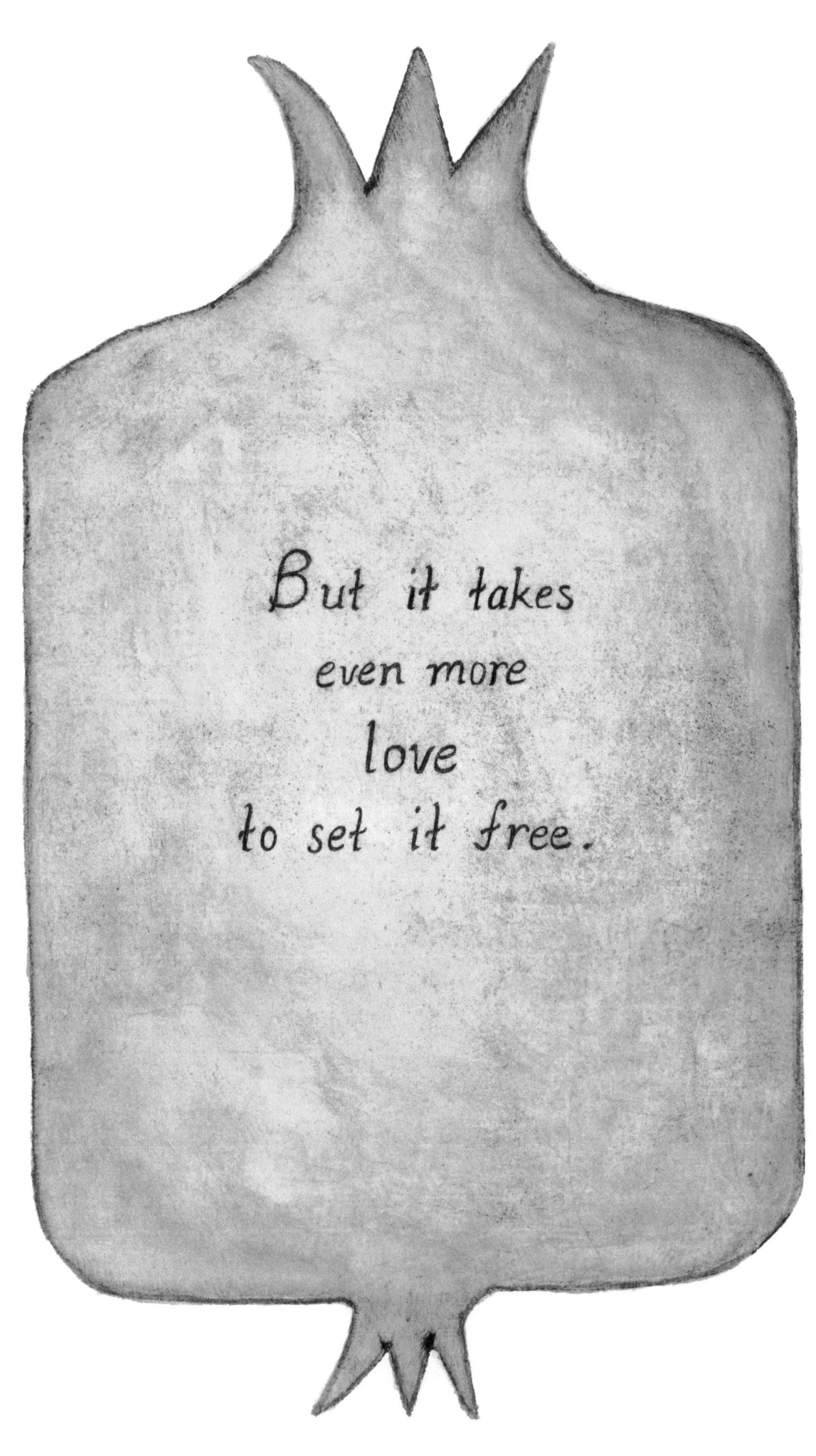

But it takes
even more
love
to set it free.

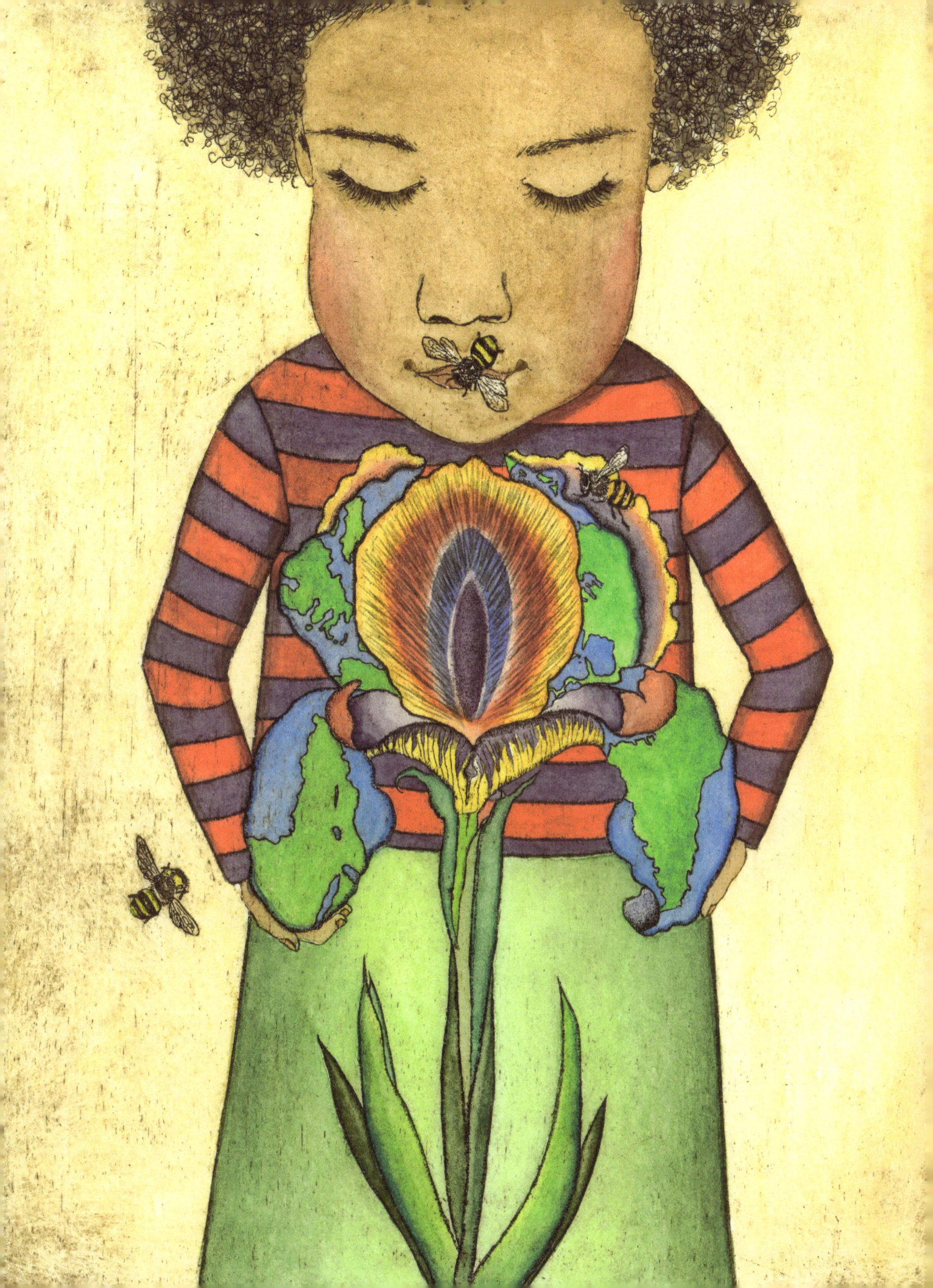

And when you do,
you will find
where
all the love in the world
has
always been...

...in you, my princess!

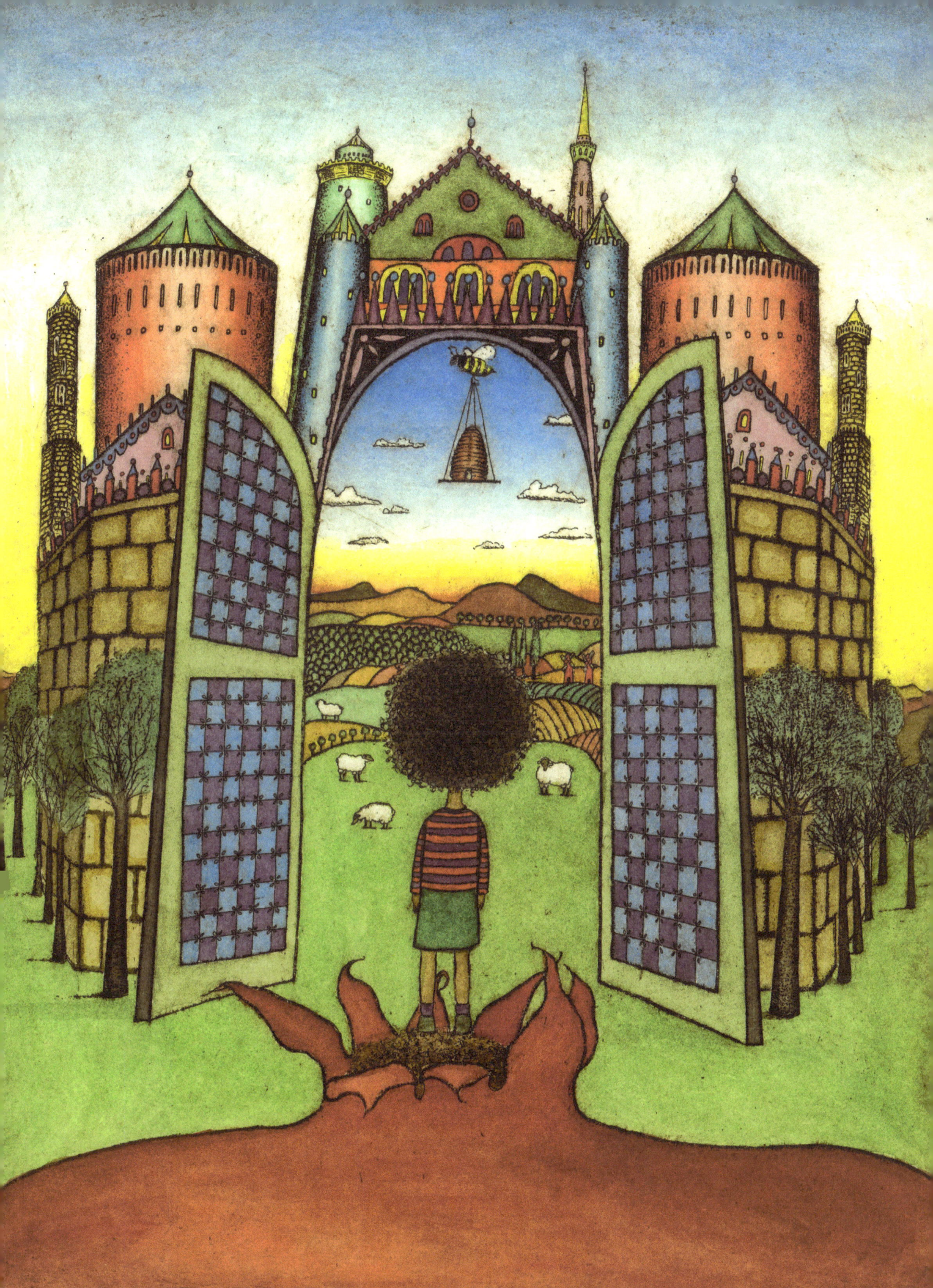

Copyright © 2009 by Vartouhi B. Pinkston

www.ingramcontent.com/pod-product-compliance
Lightning Source LLC
Chambersburg PA
CBHW041305180526

45172CB00003B/981